www.victorpublishing.co.uk

ISBN: 9798692549938

Cricket Alphabet

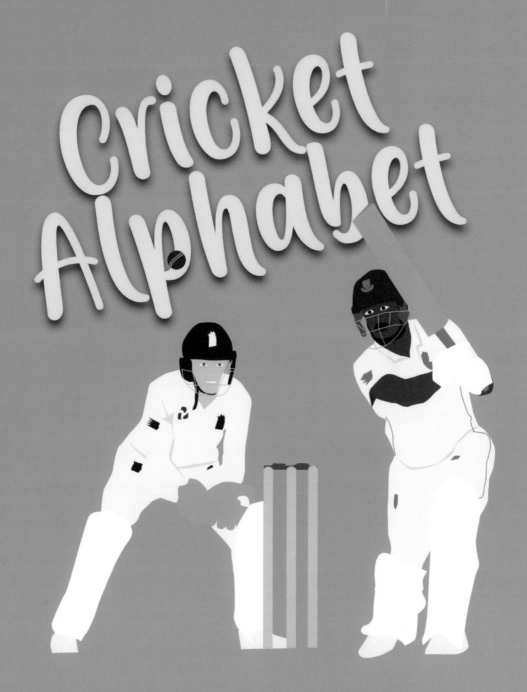

WRITTEN BY
Phil Brennan

ILLUSTRATED BY
Ric Pennington

A is for Appeal

for an in or an out

C is for Catch

before the ball hits the floor

D is for Duck

a batter has failed to score

E is for Eleven

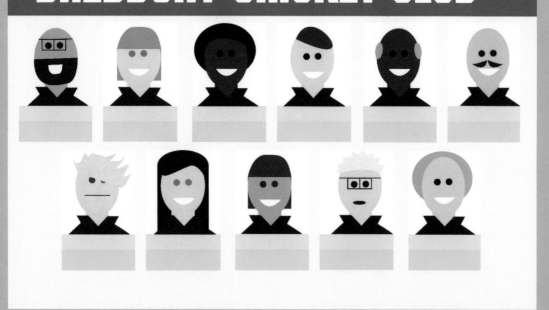

BREDBURY CRICKET CLUB

players on each team for a game

F

is for Fielders

stopping runs is the aim

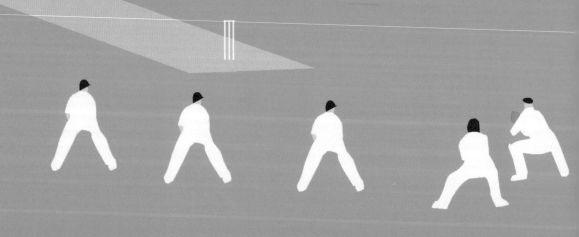

G
is for
Gloves

to help wicketkeepers catch the ball

H

is for HOWZAT

the appeal heard
most of all

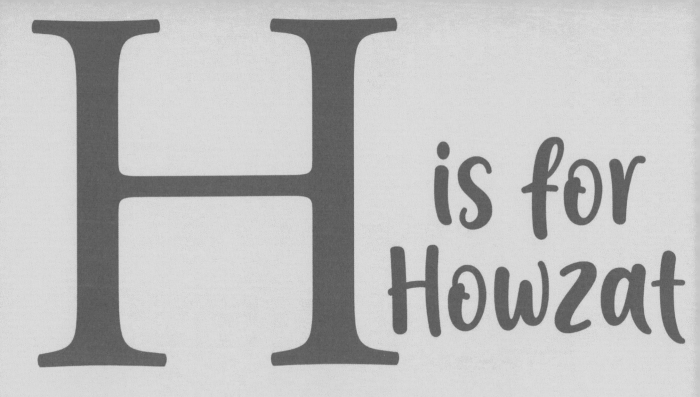

HOWZAT

I is for In

when the batters perform

J

is for Jumper

worn when the weather's not warm

K is for knock

TOTAL	208
WKTS	3
OVERS	38

a good score
there's no doubt

L

is for Leg

before wicket, gets many batters out

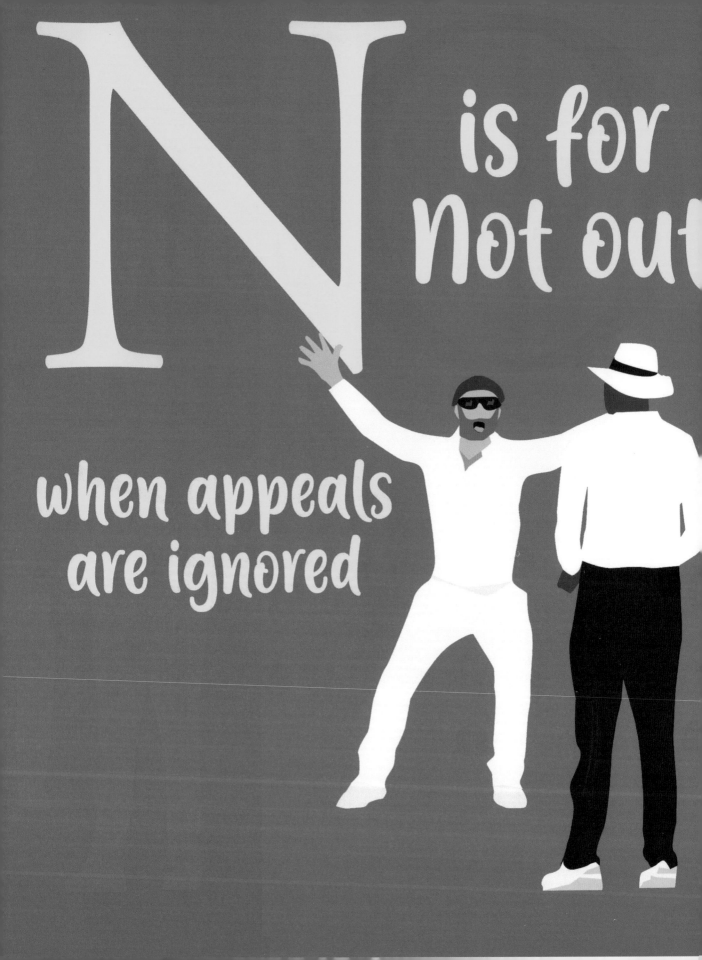

O is for Over

when six balls have been bowled

P is for Pitch

which has been neatly rolled

Q is for
Quick
bowling

which often
wins the
day

R is for Rain

which when heavy stops play

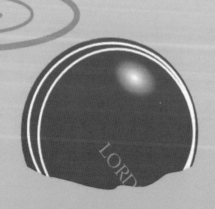

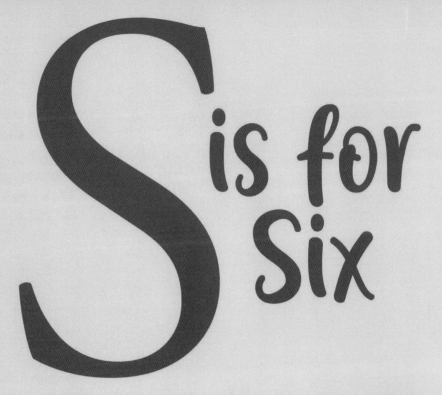

S is for Six

a strike of the ball
that scores best .

U is for Umpire

by whom decisions are made

V is for Village

where much cricket is played

W

is for Wicket

bowlers want them to fall

X

is for
X-ray

needed when hit
by the ball

Y is for Yorker

a ball that batters find hard to play

Z is for Zzzzzzz

sweet dreams
after a very
enjoyable
day

Victor PUBLISHING

Also available...

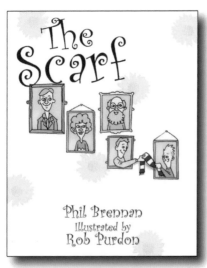

The Scarf
A beautifully illustrated, fun journey through history, as generations of football fans pass their team's scarf down through the family.

Tangerine Dream
A wonderful rhyming tale that takes a humourous look through the history of Blackpol FC

What If I Don't Make It?
The tale of a little boy who wants to make it as a footballer but is hindered by his inability to play the beautiful game

Ben and the Magic Boots
When Ben's grandad gives him a pair of his old football boots, magical things happen on the pitch.

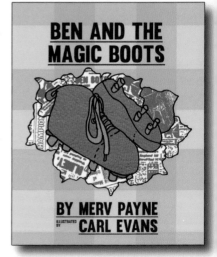

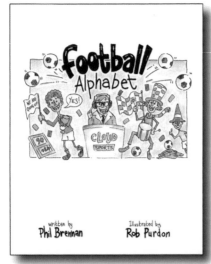

Granny's Galactic Garden
Twins Tilly and Karl discover that the old bus shelter in their Granny's garden is the starting place for some extra-terrestrial adventures...

Football Alphabet
A humorously illustrated journey of the beautiful game from A to Z

amazon

ALL TITLES AVAILABLE AT: victorpublishing.co.uk and amazon.co.uk